THE PETTYS

Triumphs & Tragedies of Auto Racing's First Family

BY

MARK STEWART

THE MILLBROOK PRESS
BROOKFIELD, CONNECTICUT

M

THE MILLBROOK PRESS

Produced by
BITTERSWEET PUBLISHING
John Sammis, President
and
TEAM STEWART, INC.

Series Design and Electronic Page Makeup by
JAFFE ENTERPRISES
Ron Jaffe

Researched and Edited by Mike Kennedy

All photos courtesy AP/ Wide World Photos, Inc. except the following:
Tom Copeland, News & Record — Cover (image of Petty family)
Daytona Racing Archives — Pages 7, 9
Bittersweet Publishing, Inc. — Pages 10, 16, 17, 30, 42, 43, 44
The following images are from the collection of Team Stewart:
Old Car — Page 2
Pro Set, Inc. — Pages 13 (© 1991), 32 (© 1991), 37 (© 1991)
Mark Stewart — Page 20 (© 2000)
Traks Race Products — Page 23 (©1991)
NASCAR Inc. — Page 36 (© 1972)
T. G. Racing, Inc. — Page 41 (© 1991)
St. Martin's Press — Page 48 (© 1993)
Sprint — Page 53 bottom (© 2001)
Beckett Publications, Inc. — Page 54 (© 1995)

Printed in the United States of America

Published by
The Millbrook Press, Inc.
2 Old New Milford Road
Brookfield, Connecticut 06804

www.millbrookpress.com

Library of Congress Cataloging-in-Publication Data

Stewart, Mark.
  The Pettys : triumphs & tragedies of auto racing's first family / Mark Stewart.
  p. cm.
  Includes index.
  ISBN 0-7613-2273-6 (lib. bdg.)
  1. Petty family. 2. Automobile racing drivers—United States—Biography. I. Title.
GV1032.A1 S74 2001
796.72'092'273—dc21
[B]
                                                                    00-066823

1 3 5 7 9 10 8 6 4 2

CONTENTS

A FAMILY THING

"I really don't know what the family did before stock-car racing was invented."

Richard Petty

Family is everything. It is all you have when you start in life, and what you most hope to have when you finish. Your family is *who* you are and where you are *from*. It shapes you and tests you. And it is the chain that links you to everyone who has come before you, and everyone who will come after.

A family *business* works because it brings together the talent and dedication of people working toward a common cause: improving life for the family. The oldest members provide experience and wisdom, while the youngest contribute fresh ideas and hard work. As each generation grows old and leaves the business, a new one takes its place. Some of the most well known and successful companies in the world are family businesses. Many of the companies in your town are family businesses, too.

In the world of auto racing, the most celebrated family business belongs to the Petty family. Their story stretches across many decades. It is about winning and losing, hard

Richard Petty's total of 200 career victories stands as one of the most remarkable records in all of sports. He says that, without his family, there is no way he would have won a single race.

Automobile racing was still a young sport when a Petty first climbed behind the wheel of a fast car, but Daytona Beach—future home of the famous Daytona 500—was already well established. Pictured above is the winner of the 1906 100-mile race there.

times and good times, great triumphs and unspeakable tragedies. It is about giving your life to a sport that does not always give back.

The story of the Petty family really gets into gear in the years following World War II. America was a land of opportunity. During the 1940s, the country had developed the technology and the confidence to accomplish anything. Now, in peacetime, industry was humming, jobs were plentiful, everyone seemed to have money in their pockets, and stores were full of great stuff for people to buy. No one could remember a time when the future looked brighter.

Not everyone shared in this spectacular abundance, however. Lee Petty, like many in rural North Carolina, was not part of the economic "mainstream." He had to do a little of everything in order to make ends meet.

DID YOU KNOW?

The Petty "compound" at Level Cross originally belonged to Lee's in-laws. He raised his family in a smaller house on the property that lacked many of the basics. "I was 12 years old before we had electricity in the house!" Richard remembers.

Lee's family had lived around Randleman, in the western part of the state, for nearly 200 years. For generations, the Pettys had been earnest and resourceful workers. Lee's father, Judson Petty, certainly was no stranger to hard work. He grew a little tobacco on the family farm, cut and hauled some lumber, worked on car and tractor engines, raised hogs, drove a taxi and a watermelon truck, and even ran a small trucking company.

Lee grew up doing the same things Petty boys had for generations. He hunted, fished, explored, and learned how to do everything his father did. Lee especially liked to race. He would take on all challengers—on foot or on bicycle. He was not always the fastest or the strongest, but he almost always found a way to win. As Lee liked to say, "There is no second place. You either win or lose. That's the only two parts there are to racing."

Lee married young. He was just 17 when he walked down the aisle in 1931, and by the end of the 1930s he and Elizabeth had two boys, Richard (1937) and Maurice (1938). The Great Depression was hard on the Pettys, but Lee's skill as a truck driver and mechanic helped him succeed where others might have given up. When Maurice contracted polio, the family was further burdened. But in the "race" of life, Lee was determined to be a winner.

With his competitive spirit and mechanical know-how, it was only a matter of time before Lee Petty was drawn to the dirt-track auto races that flourished in the South during the 1940s.

> *"One thing my daddy taught me is don't get above your upbringing."*
> RICHARD PETTY

Many in the backwoods of North Carolina resorted to "moonshining"—manufacturing and selling liquor illegally. Lee wanted no part of this dangerous life, although he was friendly with several moonshiners and may have worked on their cars. A fast, dependable car was everything to these outlaws. Once the liquor was bottled, it had to be transported to customers. Local police would lie in wait for the moonshiners and then pursue them on wild high-speed chases in the middle of the night. A slow car, or an unreliable car, could get you caught. Or it could get you killed.

The most successful moonshiners became local celebrities. Their "fans" would debate endlessly about who was the best driver or who owned the fastest car. Often these arguments would be settled head-to-head, late at night, on long stretches of country roads. Lee could not resist entering these illegal drag races. Soon, he was acknowledged as one of the best drivers in North Carolina.

By 1946, these contests had moved to dirt ovals and involved a dozen or more cars at a time. Spectators were charged a quarter or 50 cents to attend the races, with part of the money handed over to the winning driver. After attending a few of these races, Lee and his brother, Julie, decided to enter a car. Lee won his first race, finished second in his second race, and finished third in his third race. He was in love with the sport,

Lee, right, with fellow racer Jim Reed, left, and NASCAR president Bill France.
Both drivers were fan favorites during the early 1950s.

but realized he was at a disadvantage. The "pros"(the moonshiners) could afford to send away for special parts to make their cars faster. Lee could barely afford the gas money. He soon had no choice but to pull out of racing.

Lee and his boys continued to attend races whenever they could. In February 1948, he took Richard and Maurice down to Daytona Beach, Florida, to watch the big race

The house at Level Cross,
where the Petty dynasty began

there. The hard-packed sand allowed cars to pick up tremendous speed on the straightaways, then gave way in the turns, creating thrilling "fishtails" as the drivers tried desperately to control their vehicles.

There Lee encountered Bill France, the sport's most popular promoter. France wanted to take racing out of the hands of slick, unscrupulous promoters, who sometimes left town with the gate receipts before paying off the drivers. He also wanted to change the sport's image.

France's idea was to move away from the moonshiner image and appeal more to the South's growing middle class. To accomplish this, he decided that the cars on the track should be identical to the ones people saw in dealership showrooms. No special parts or modifications would be allowed. If a good mechanic could coax a little more power out of a "stock" car, and a good driver could outmaneuver his opponents,

then that car deserved to cross the finish line first. He called his organization NASCAR, which stood for the National Association of Stock Car Auto Racing.

This concept appealed to Lee Petty. Behind the wheel and under the hood, he believed he had no equal.

DID YOU KNOW?

The Petty competitiveness coursed through the entire family—and was not always limited to the track. After a race in which the gigantic "Tiny" Lund edged Lee, Richard (still just a kid) and his mother went after Lund as he mounted the winner's stand. After a brief shouting match, Elizabeth started clobbering him with her purse and skinny Richard jumped on his back when Lund tried to defend himself. The good-natured Lund shook them off and sprinted away, laughing.

RUNNING TOUGH, RUNNING SMART

chapter **2**

"There were times when I was getting started in racing when we hardly had enough money to buy the groceries."

Lee Petty

In June 1949, NASCAR's first all-stock car race was held in Charlotte, North Carolina, on a dirt course less than a mile around. Lee Petty drove in that historic 150-mile race. Richard, 12, and Maurice, 11, worked the pits for their father with their mother cheering them on.

Every penny was precious. Lee entered the family car, a 1946 Buick Roadmaster. As they neared the Charlotte Speedway, he stopped at a gas station, put the car on a hydraulic lift, and "set it up" for the race.

"When my daddy started out, there wasn't money to be made."

RICHARD PETTY

Lee had plenty to smile about after his first Grand National win, in 1949.

The Pettys stayed together in a tiny tourist cabin and ate food they had packed before leaving home.

On the race's 107th lap, Lee pushed his heavy Buick a little too hard going into the third turn. His family watched in horror as he rolled over and over, destroying the car. Lee climbed out with a cut on his cheek. While Elizabeth was fretting about how they would find their way home, Lee was wondering where he could lay his hands on a lighter, more maneuverable race car!

Lee scraped up some cash, bought a used Plymouth, and brought it back to the house in Level Cross. There he and his sons worked in the family "garage." It was a flimsy wooden roof held up by four cedar poles, where they also butchered hogs. Lee drove the Plymouth to a pair of second-place finishes before winning his first NASCAR race, in Pittsburgh, Pennsylvania. The winner's check was $1,500. This brought his first-year earnings to $3,855. Lee ended the season ranked second, behind Red Byron.

FIRST RACE

When the Pettys issued their own set of cards in the 1990s, collectors snapped up this one of Richard working in his dad's garage. Thanks to Lee's success, the family could afford to put Richard behind the wheel. "I came along during the best part of his career as far as making money," says Richard. "And it gave him the leeway to let me have a car. If he had had bad seasons and hadn't been winning races, and if there had been no money, I might still be working on cars."

Lee soon became a regular on the circuit. Unlike the other top drivers, he did not make a lot of money from sponsors. Lee preferred to run his own show; he liked to call the shots. Still, he finished among the top money winners each year during the early 1950s. "Daddy's probably the smartest driver who ever lived," claims Richard, "because he did it all himself. He drove, he worked on the car, he called the shots on pit strategy—and as far as speed is concerned, he won with inferior equipment."

Indeed, Lee Petty actually plotted out his races assuming that everyone else *had* a better car. He would tuck himself away behind the leaders, a lap or two down, concentrating on running smoothly and staying out of trouble. Then he would wait for that inevitable opportunity: a spinout, a crash, a sloppy pit stop, or some other

> **DID YOU KNOW?**
>
> In stock-car racing's early years, few drivers competed past the age of 30. That made Lee Petty easy to spot—he was a good 10 years older than almost anyone on the track.

miscalculation. Then Lee would make his move. Sometimes he would win, sometimes he would not. But he would almost always finish among the leaders.

The other drivers thought of Lee as being "dirty." In racing talk, that meant that he would sneak up on you when you least expected it, or that he would try to do things that would wear down the front-runners. The freewheeling stars of the old days, such

Curtis Turner, left, was both friend and foe to Lee Petty.
Like Lee, he won one of the eight NASCAR stock events in 1949.

as Curtis Turner, Herb Thomas, and Tim and Fonty Flock, preferred to go fender-to-fender with the guys they had to beat. They did not want to admit it, but Lee was just driving smart. If a situation called for it, Lee Petty had no problem scraping metal with a competitor. "If he had to lay a fender on you, he would," remembers Richard. "But if it wasn't necessary, he wouldn't."

Lee understood NASCAR's scoring system better than anyone else. Drivers were awarded a certain number of points based on where they finished a race, and those points would be added to their totals in the Grand National standings. At the end of the year, the driver with the most points—not necessarily the most victories—was crowned champion. If Lee saw a chance to win a race, he would seize it. But if he did not, he would not take any chances and be satisfied with second- or third- or fourth-place points. In 1954, Herb Thomas won 12 events and Lee took seven. However, Lee also recorded 25 Top 10 finishes in the season's remaining 27 races to edge Thomas 8,649 points to 8,366 and win his first title.

Edging Herb Thomas, left, for the driving championship in 1954
was not easy for Lee. Thomas was the greatest dirt-track driver ever.

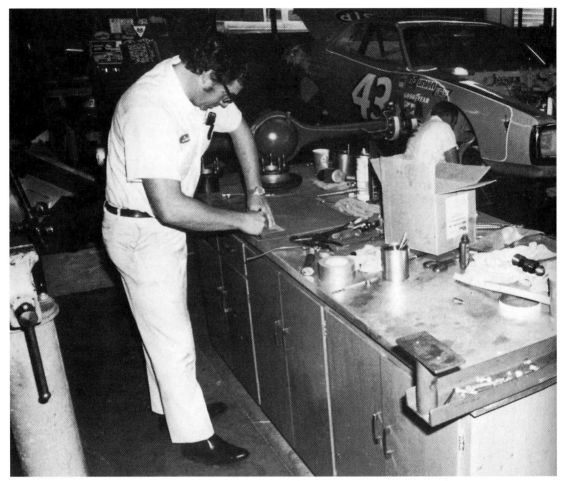

Dale Inman, cousin to Maurice and Richard, joined the Petty team in the 1950s.
He served as mechanic in Richard's first race.

Fame did not bring fortune to the Pettys. Lee was lucky if he could bank more than 10 percent of what he won. And the boys had to chip in and work hard, both at the races and at home. "When we first started, I went to school, came home at night, and worked on the cars," Richard says. "My ambition was to be a good mechanic, to be able to build a race car and pit race cars. I never really thought about driving until I got out of high school."

After finishing either third or fourth the next three seasons, Lee reclaimed the top spot in 1958. He was no longer driving the little Plymouths. In 1957, Lee had made a deal to get an Oldsmobile and started blowing everyone away. The Olds was a far superior automobile to the Plymouth. The best car plus the best mind equaled victory after victory. Lee quickly surged to the top of the all-time win list.

By this time Richard was getting the racing bug. He had first asked his father about driving when he was 17, but Lee told him not until he was 21. "When daddy said no, that was that," says Richard.

In July 1958, Richard again asked Lee if he could race. This time the answer was yes. "He said, 'Yeah, okay, there's a car. Go get it, fix it up, and take it to the race.' It was a 1957 Oldsmobile convertible."

While Lee was competing in Asheville, North Carolina, Richard ran his first race in Columbia, South Carolina, with cousin Dale Inman as his mechanic. He finished sixth in a special event for convertibles. "I can remember running that first race," he recalls, "and saying to myself, 'Man, this is what I want to do.'"

A couple of weeks later, at an event in Toronto, Canada, Richard entered one of Lee's backup cars in his first official Grand National event. He painted a "1" in front of Lee's

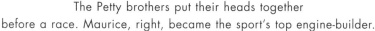

The Petty brothers put their heads together before a race. Maurice, right, became the sport's top engine-builder.

well-known "42" and proceeded to crash the car through a fence on the 55th lap. The driver who pushed him off the track was Lee, who went on to win the race. "I found out real quick how much I didn't know about driving a race car," laughs Richard.

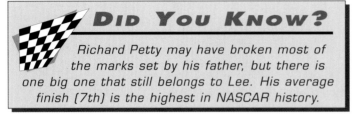

DID YOU KNOW?

Richard Petty may have broken most of the marks set by his father, but there is one big one that still belongs to Lee. His average finish (7th) is the highest in NASCAR history.

The next day Richard took the team's third car, numbered it "42-A," and entered another event. This time he finished without incident. As Richard gravitated toward driving, Maurice began to show a special talent for working on cars. He and his cousin Dale formed the "nuts and bolts" portion of the Petty racing team.

"I didn't win anything in the first couple of years," says Richard. "I spent a lot of my father's money on racing cars. But he never said anything about it. He just let me find my own way in the sport."

Lee was now the grand old man of stock-car racing. He had just the right mix of fear and respect from the other drivers, and he was the sport's supreme strategist. In 1959, Lee became NASCAR's first back-to-back champion, winning a career-best 11 races and finishing second or third a total of 12 times. His season still ranks among the most dominant ever, in any sport. The sum of all the prize money earned by the second- through sixth-ranked drivers that year was just a few dollars more than Lee won all by himself.

Lee's competitive fire was evident in Atlanta that year, at Lakewood Speedway. Richard took the checkered flag (his first in Grand National competition) but was denied the win when the second-place finisher lodged a protest, claiming Richard had been mistakenly credited with an extra lap. Race officials took away Richard's first win and gave it to the runner-up—you guessed it—Lee Petty.

LEE

BY THE NUMBERS

STARTS	427
WINS	54
TOP 10s	332
CHAMPIONSHIPS	3
CAREER EARNINGS	$237,337

"Daddy said I'd probably win some more races later," Richard recalls.

PHOTO FINISH

For many years, Daytona Beach, Florida, had been one of the hot spots of American auto racing. That made it the perfect place for racing's most ambitious idea: a thoroughly modern 2.5 mile "superspeedway." The track opened in February of 1959 and played host to history's first Daytona 500. Bill France had gambled millions that stock-car racing was ready to become a big-time sport, and he needed a big-time finish to splash across the nation's sports pages. Lee Petty and Johnny Beauchamp gave it to him, breaking out of a tight pack at the three-quarter mark and dueling back and forth the rest of the way.

The two cars crossed the finish line together. Lee glanced over and felt he had won by a few inches, but the race was awarded to Beauchamp. "We were going to head back home," remembers Richard. "Then we thought, 'No, we better stay here in Daytona.'"

It was a good decision. Many at the finish line agreed with the Pettys. After 40 hours, newsreel films flown down from New York proved conclusively that Lee had nosed out Beauchamp. France had his fantastic finish, and stock-car racing had a new jewel in its crown, the Daytona 500.

SON OF A GUN

chapter **3**

"I never entered a race in my life I didn't try to win."

Richard Petty

Richard Petty got his first official NASCAR win a year later, in Charlotte. "When everybody else broke down, we won," he says modestly. The truth is that he outdrove three Hall of Famers (Lee Petty, Ned Jarrett, and Joe Weatherly) and that year's Grand National Champion (Rex White). At 23, Richard was already well liked and respected for his modesty and low-key approach to the sport.

Richard's 1960 season was an excellent one. He won two more races and came in second six times.

DID YOU KNOW?

Richard may hold the record for most autographs signed in a lifetime. His signature may also be the most elaborate and beautiful. He uses his entire arm instead of just his hand, to keep from getting writer's cramp.

Richard in 1960, the year he won his first event, in Charlotte. Lee finished second in the race.

In 40 starts, he turned in a remarkable 40 Top 10 finishes. That was good enough for second place on the NASCAR point list. Lee, with five wins, finished the year sixth. Going into the 1961 season, racing fans had every reason to expect a changing of the guard in the Petty family. No one could have foreseen how quickly, or violently, that change would come.

Prior to the 1961 Daytona 500, in one of the event's preliminary races, Richard spun out, crashed through a barrier, and got a face full of broken glass. While doctors carefully picked the pieces out, Richard listened to the remainder of the race on the radio. What he heard made him sick to his stomach. While trying to avoid another car that had spun out, Lee and Johnny Beauchamp crashed through the guardrail at 150 mph. This was not one of the old dirt tracks, where an unlucky driver might end up nose-down in a pigsty. Daytona was one of the new superspeedways, with high-banked turns. Lee's car sailed through the air, turned over, and came to rest wheels-up in a parking lot almost 200 feet away.

The Petty Enterprises brain trust ruled stock-car racing in the 1960s. Lee, flanked by Maurice and Richard, stopped racing after a 1961 crash left him disabled.

Richard Petty **TRAKS**

> *"I was lucky in a way that the first stars of NASCAR were all nearing the end of their careers when I came up. . . . And I was lucky that the superspeedways like Daytona were just getting built when I came along. . . . I could grow along with the sport."*
>
> RICHARD PETTY, PICTURED ON HIS FINAL CARD AS AN ACTIVE DRIVER.

By the time Richard reached the scene, his father had been whisked away by an ambulance. (Beauchamp was fine.) "I ran down the bank and saw what was left of the car," recalls Richard. "There was blood all over the place and people said he was dead for sure. I thought he was dead, too."

Although he lost tremendous amounts of blood, Lee pulled through with a broken collarbone, punctured lung, and shattered leg. When he limped out of the hospital four months later, he was wearing a leg brace that he would keep the remainder of his life. Lee drove in six more races over the next three years, but he knew his racing days were through. From now on Richard would do the the racing, Maurice would be the crew chief, and Lee would run Petty Enterprises.

With the spotlight now on Richard, racing fans began to see that he had learned well from his father. He had the same terrific patience as the old man, knowing when to hang back and when to charge ahead. However, Richard was more artistic. Anyone who knew anything about racing could see he had

DID YOU KNOW?

The secret of Richard's success at the 1964 Daytona 500 was a simple two-by-four. Nailed to the right side of his seat, it prevented his bottom from sliding when he took turns at 190 mph—enabling him to apply consistent pressure to the gas pedal throughout the race.

a subtle "touch" in the corners, and the experts marveled at his ability to drive high on the track. Most drivers prefer to do their work in the first or second lane of the big

> **"When Richard sneaks in behind you, you can hardly feel it."**
>
> A. J. FOYT

tracks. Richard usually stayed in the third lane, swooping down only to pass.

Richard was a hit with the fans off the track, too. Often he would spend the tense moments prior to a race chitchatting with the crowd, signing autographs, and answering questions about his car. He was gentle and soft-spoken and really made a connection with the people. He was not flashy, yet he had a magnetic personality. Even the old-time drivers liked him. No one knew it then, but Richard would become the most famous stock-car racer of his generation—and the next one, as well!

After finishing eighth overall in 1961, Richard turned in a pair of magnificent seasons in 1962 and 1963. He won a total of 22 races, and finished a close second to Joe Weatherly both years. Richard was great on the short tracks, but his talents were diminished somewhat by the larger ovals, where raw speed and risk-taking often added up to victory. In 1964, Richard achieved his first win in a superspeedway event when he captured the Daytona 500. He went on that year to win eight more races and finished second or third another

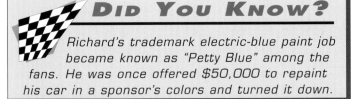

DID YOU KNOW?

Richard's trademark electric-blue paint job became known as "Petty Blue" among the fans. He was once offered $50,000 to repaint his car in a sponsor's colors and turned it down.

26 times to take his first Grand National championship. In a decade when the measure of sports superstardom was the $100,000 salary, Richard became just the second stock-car driver ever to reach that plateau.

Richard shows off his trophy for winning the 1964 Daytona 500.

PEDAL TO THE METAL

chapter 4

"Some of the good boys only run the big ones, but our approach is to run 'em all."

Lee Petty

After Richard Petty's super 1964 season, Bill France began getting complaints about the engine the Pettys were using. The powerful "hemi-head" design by Chrysler—especially in the hands of Maurice and Lee—was far superior to those made by other companies and used by other drivers. Another hemi engine prepared by Maurice, in Jim Paschal's Plymouth, won the 1964 World 600 in Charlotte.

Over the years, France had relaxed the rules about what was a "stock" car and what was not. Technically, the engine in question was not made for street vehicles. The hemi, claimed critics, could not be found in the local car showroom, so why should it be allowed on the track? Fearing that automotive giant Ford Motor Company might pull out of stock-car racing rather than risk another season of embarrassment, France agreed to ban hemi engines.

Bill France was the biggest man in NASCAR, but Richard battled him
to a standoff in 1965 when Petty Enterprises' Chrysler engines came under attack.

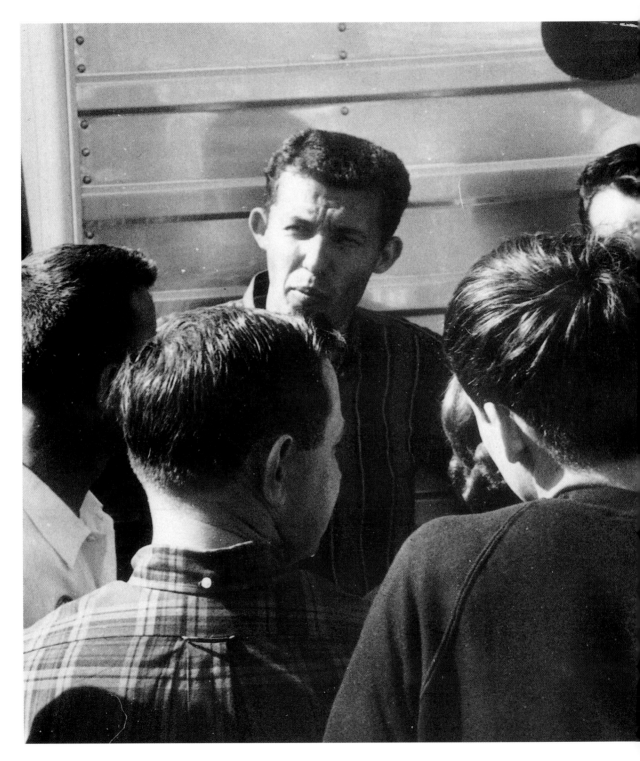

DID YOU KNOW?

Superstar A. J. Foyt, right, competed occasionally in stock-car events. He was the one driver Richard would have liked to face more often. "If Foyt had run with us full-time, nobody might have ever heard of Richard Petty. Then again, nobody might have ever heard of A. J. Foyt!"

Chrysler took this news badly. With no suitable engine to replace the hemi, the company decided to pull all of its sponsorship money out of stock-car racing. As you can imagine, this development caught the Pettys by surprise. After considering their options, Petty Enterprises determined that if stock-car racing did not want the sport's biggest star, someone else would. Lee, Maurice, and Richard decided to get into the drag-racing business!

What seemed like a fun idea turned tragic, however, when Richard's dragster swerved out of control and entered the crowd at a drag strip in Dallas, Georgia. A little boy was killed, not much older than Richard's five-year-old son, Kyle. It was a memory he would never be able to shake.

The pain and shock are still evident on Richard's face
after the drag-strip accident that killed a young spectator in 1965.

The garage at a stock-car race is packed with drivers and mechanics. It was in these close quarters that Richard earned the friendship and respect of his rivals.

Realizing his grave error, France moved to reinstate the hemi engine that summer. On August 19, 1965, Chrysler (and the Pettys) were back in the NASCAR fold. In the 14 races that remained, Richard won four times and finished in the Top 10 in the rest.

Drivers had tested Bill France's authority in the past—and been punished severely. To racing fans, it looked as if Richard had stood up to the king of stock cars and won. Was power shifting from the people who staged the races to the people who won them? Of course, there was more to the story than that, but it would not be long before the sport would have a new "king." The first step toward auto racing's unofficial throne came in the first race of the 1966 season. Richard, behind the wheel of familiar car 43, became the first driver to win the Daytona 500 twice. He finished the year with a total of eight Grand National victories.

The next step for Richard was to break stock-car racing's most cherished record. In 1955, Tim Flock dominated the Grand National circuit, winning 18 races. In the years that followed, others threatened this mark, but the closest anyone had come was 16. In 1967, Richard shot past 18 wins, finishing with an astonishing 27 victories, including 10 straight.

Every sport has one crazy statistic, a record so amazing that it almost seems impossible. Baseball's is Mark McGwire and his 70 homers; football's is Dan Marino's 48

Richard's 27 victories in 1967 put him in fast company.
Here he poses with international racing legend Andy Granatelli.

PRO SET RACING

43

429 C.I.

429 C.I. TORINO COBRA EAST TENN Ford

43

FORD BY PETTY

"The good drivers just know when to pass and when not to, when to charge and when to hang back, and, most important, how much their car can take on that day and that track."

RICHARD PETTY

PICTURED IN HIS PETTY-BLUE 1969 FORD, WHICH WAS COMMEMORATED IN A 1991 TRADING CARD.

touchdown passes; basketball's is Wilt Chamberlain's 100 points in a game; hockey's is Wayne Gretzky's 215 points. Auto racing's is Richard Petty's 27 wins in 1967. This number defies logic and reason. And it probably will never be broken.

After a slow beginning, the 1967 season turned into one of those magical runs. Almost everything went right. Richard won twice in his first nine starts, then took 10 of the next 16 events. After four wins in New York and New Jersey on the northeast swing, Richard grabbed the checkered flag in 11 of the next 12 races, including a record 10 in a row.

Richard and his blue Plymouth were in perfect harmony. In the pits and back in the garage, Maurice and Lee could do no wrong. Petty Enterprises entered every race expecting to win, while the other teams seemed resigned to competing for second place. At the start of the year, Richard had 48 career victories. He

RICHARD

BY THE NUMBERS

STARTS	1,184
WINS	200
TOP 10s	712
CHAMPIONSHIPS	7
CAREER EARNINGS	$8,541,218

became the sport's all-time leader when he notched number 55, surpassing his dad for the top spot.

By *any* measure, he was now the undisputed king of the stock cars.

HERE'S THE DEAL

It is very expensive to run a racing team. Even the Pettys—who won more races than anyone, and whose key workers were family members—would have gone broke had they relied solely on prize money to pay their bills. Where does the money come from? Companies pay team owners for putting their names and logos on cars and for drivers to wear their patches. The more races a team wins, the more money they can charge. Also, the top teams get money and technical support from car manufacturers, who want their vehicles to lead as many laps and win as many races as possible. If a Ford wins a big race, for instance, it is not unusual for sales of Fords to rise sharply. When television came into the sport, the money available for sponsorships rose sharply. Today, cars and drivers are completely covered with corporate logos.

David Pearson, the man Richard saw in his rear-view mirror more than any other

CHALLENGES TO THE THRONE

chapter 5

"We finished one–two more than anybody else ever did."

David Pearson

When an athlete has a completely dominant season, as Richard Petty did in 1967, a sport can sometimes suffer. Fans get tired of watching the same person win over and over again, and they look for entertainment elsewhere. What racing fans needed was a worthy rival for the King. In 1968, they got one. His name was David Pearson, and he matched Richard win-for-win throughout the season.

Pearson was hardly a newcomer. He followed Richard as Rookie of the Year in 1960 and won a remarkable 15 races in 1966 to take the Grand National championship. Richard considered

DID YOU KNOW?

David Pearson may have been Richard's biggest rival, but during the early 1970s Richard and Bobby Allison engaged in one of history's great fender-bending feuds. Finally, in 1972, the two called a truce, and have been good friends ever since.

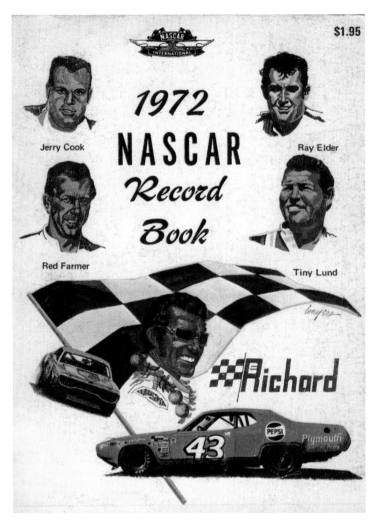

$1.95

NASCAR INTERNATIONAL

1972 NASCAR *Record Book*

Jerry Cook

Ray Elder

Red Farmer

Tiny Lund

Richard

PEPSI
Plymouth
43

Richard's 21-win season in 1971 earned him and his Petty-blue Plymouth the cover of the 1972 NASCAR guide.

Pearson the best driver in the sport, for he could adjust his style to any size and type of track. During the 1968 season, both drivers won 16 races and earned 12 "poles" for the fastest pre-race qualifying time. But it was Pearson who won the points battle. In 1969, Richard was edged again by Pearson, who finished first, second, or third an astonishing 38 times. Over the next 15 years, they would have many memorable duels.

"Pearson could beat you on a short track, he could beat you on a super-speedway, he could beat you on a road course, he could beat you on a dirt track," says Richard. "It didn't hurt as bad to lose to Pearson as it did to lose to some of the others, because I knew how good he was."

The 1970 season saw Petty Enterprises field two sleek, futuristic Plymouth "Superbirds." These cars featured big airfoils and hemi engines built by Maurice, and they wreaked havoc on the competition. Richard won 18 races, while Teddy Enterprises teammate Pete Hamilton drove to victory at the Daytona 500 and two other races. The Superbirds were outlawed in 1971, but Richard hardly missed a beat. He drove to 21 victories and finished as the the top-ranked driver.

This card was the first to picture Lee, Maurice, and Richard together

A THIRD CHAMPIONSHIP

Because of a new law preventing cigarette companies from advertising on television, a lot of money was suddenly available to sponsor high-profile events. Winston cigarettes and its parent company, R. J. Reynolds Tobacco, decided to plow its money into stock-car racing. So in 1971, the Grand National series was renamed the "Winston Cup." That made Richard the first Winston Cup champion in history.

No one would ever win 20 races in a season again. Thanks in large part to the Pettys, stock-car racing was ready to move ahead and become a "major-league" sport, and that meant eliminating some of its "minor-league" tracks. Fans were sad to see them go. Some had been with NASCAR since the very beginning. But Bill France and his son, Bill France Jr., wanted bigger and better tracks to attract more fans and accommodate an increasingly important "partner"—television.

Over the next decade, stock-car racing changed dramatically. More and more people attended races and watched on TV. More and more companies paid driving teams to put their stickers and patches on their cars and uniforms. Team owners had a lot more money to work with. As a result, the business of racing became much more sophisticated. What was once "guesswork" could now be tested with computers and wind tunnels. Where experience and intuition had once ruled the day, physics and calculus now played a major role.

These enormous changes did not figure to help the Pettys. They had stayed ahead doing things the old-fashioned way. Lee Petty, for one, was not interested in high-tech racing. He turned the business over to his sons and spent most of his time playing golf. Not surprisingly, he became very good very fast. Maurice Petty welcomed the extra money and the cutting-edge technology. Although Petty Enterprises' competitors would have access to the same new gadgets and gizmos, he and Richard figured they would find a way to squeeze a little more out of the same equipment.

Richard waves to the crowd after winning the 1974 Daytona 500.

With the season trimmed down to 31 races, Richard won his second consecutive Winston Cup championship in 1972 by capturing eight races. His fourth career title set a new record. In 1973, Richard won the Daytona 500 for the fourth time. A week later, he took the checkered flag at Richmond, Virginia, for his 150th career victory.

The 1974 season began with a fifth win at Daytona and ended with a fifth championship. A few weeks after the Daytona 500, a new rule went into effect that forced the Pettys to use a smaller engine. Other drivers were complaining again that Maurice's exotic engines could not be purchased. Maurice announced that anyone with $6,500 was welcome to buy one of his engines, but he was nevertheless made to alter his design. Maurice and the Petty Enterprises team went to work and hand-built a completely new engine in three weeks. Richard promptly drove the

DID YOU KNOW?

The 1974 Daytona 500 should have been called the Daytona 450. In the midst of a crippling energy crisis, the government hinted that it might shut down gas-guzzling racing organizations if steps were not taken to conserve fuel. Bill France argued that vacationers used up far more fuel than stock-car racing, and wondered why the government was not cracking down on vacations. In accordance with federal guidelines, France trimmed the length of several races—including the Daytona 500, which was reduced by 50 miles.

car to victory at Wilkesboro. The Petty team stayed on top in 1975, winning the Winston Cup yet again.

Meanwhile the Petty-Pearson rivalry continued to generate excitement and draw more sports fans to stock-car racing. At the 1976 Daytona 500, the two cars engaged in a thrilling duel right down to the final lap. In turn four, they banged into each other and both cars spun wildly off the track just a few hundred yards short of the finish line. While the other drivers pressed hard to pick up ground and the fans screamed encouragement, the two leaders struggled to restart their cars. Pearson got his Mercury going and inched toward the finish line at 15 mph. Richard could not get his engine to turn over and sat helplessly in the infield as everyone passed him by.

Richard sits helplessly in his wrecked car as he watches David Pearson
putter across the finish line to take the checkered flag at the 1976 Daytona 500.

Helmets, fists, and feet were flying after the 1979 Daytona 500. While Richard cruised toward the victory lane, the Allison brothers, left, tangled with Cale Yarborough. The wild finish was televised live and did much to popularize stock-car racing.

Three years later, Richard was involved in another crazy finish at Daytona. The final lap featured Cale Yarborough and Donnie Allison going fender-to-fender for the victory. In turn three, they bumped, lost control, and slammed into the wall. Darting around and through the debris were Richard, young Darrell Waltrip, and superstar A. J. Foyt, all of whom had been battling for third. When these drivers realized that the two leaders were out, there

DID YOU KNOW?

Richard hated to miss a race. In 1980, he ignored doctor's orders and drove much of the season with a broken neck knowing that a jarring wreck might kill him. "If I let a race go by without racing in it, I feel like somebody's taking something away from me."

was a mad dash for the finish line. Richard beat Waltrip by a car length, with Foyt finishing third.

As Richard was motoring toward the winner's stand, a fight broke out back in turn three. Allison and Yarborough had climbed out of their twisted vehicles and were trading blows, with Donnie's brother Bobby jumping into the fray. The spectacular ending boosted stock-car racing to new heights. In the past, the Daytona 500 had been taped and replayed on television the following weekend. But in 1979, the race was being broadcast live. Millions sat with their jaws hanging open as the King streaked across the finish line, and then watched the incredible scene unfold on the infield. Those who had never witnessed a racing event believed that this was the way *every* race finished...and for the rest of the year ticket sales sky-rocketed!

Richard built on his unexpected win at Daytona to capture his seventh and final championship. It was an exciting seesaw battle all season long, with Richard winning five races and Waltrip winning seven. Richard trailed Waltrip by 17 points with three races left but won at Rockingham to retake the lead. He held on to win by a mere 11 points. It was a great finish to a landmark year.

PETTY ENTERPRISES

The Pettys' family business, Petty Enterprises, has been operating for more than 50 years. It began in 1949, when Lee Petty cleared out his reaper shed and transformed it into a garage. That tiny building still stands on the family's compound at Level Cross. In 1957, Petty Enterprises began running two cars at each event, employing Tiny Lund (pictured below on his own trading card) and Ralph Earnhardt (Dale's father). Over the years, some of the greats of auto racing have driven for the Pettys, including Joe Weatherly, Jim Paschal, Marvin Panch, Speedy Thompson, Jim Hurtubise, Buck Baker, LeeRoy Yarborough, Dan Gurney, Pete Hamilton, and John Andretti. The result is that Petty Enterprises has more races won, more poles won, and more laps led than any team in history.

TINY LUND

GENERATION K

chapter 6

"Richard Petty is probably the most popular figure in the South today."

Sam Moses — Sportswriter

The 1979 season was an important one for the Pettys and stock-car racing for another reason. It marked the beginning of Kyle Petty's Winston Cup career. In the season's 20th race, the Talladega 500, the 19-year-old got behind the wheel of car number 42 (Lee Petty's old number) and finished ninth. Kyle ran four more times that season and ended up 37th in the Winston Cup rankings.

Kyle was Richard's oldest child and only son. His three sisters, Sharon, Lisa, and

Richard with his youngest daughter, Rebecca

Young Kyle's interests ranged from gears to guitars.

Rebecca, had no interest in racing. But they were Pettys, so racing was part of their everyday life. In the spring and fall, while school was in session, the Petty kids saw their father only a few hours a week. During the summers, the four children would join the fun as Petty Enterprises visited a new track and a new city every week. Lynda Petty did her homework before each stop, locating museums, galleries, and other points of interest so her kids did not have to hang around the garage all day. Thanks mostly to his mother, Kyle was as well-rounded and cultured as a "stock-car kid" could be.

Still, Kyle was drawn to the family business. As he grew, he became more involved in what his father, uncle, and grandfather were doing. With each lesson he learned about the innards of an automobile, however, he was also being tutored on what it meant to be a Petty: hard work, dedication, devotion to the family, and always remembering who you are and where you came from. Richard also tried to tell his son that it was all right if he did not become a driver.

"Dad knew racing could be a heartbreaking existence, and that there would be tremendous pressures on me if I got into the same line of work," Kyle remembers.

DID YOU KNOW?

Kyle got his first set of wheels at the age of six, when Richard gave him a minibike. "It didn't take me long to break my fingers and get a dislocated shoulder...yet I still started to get this love for speed."

When Lee and Richard invited Kyle to "rock" with them, this might not have been what he had in mind.

"Still, deep in his heart, he wanted me to carry on what he had done, and what my grandfather had done before him."

Richard would tell Kyle again and again that just because he was a famous driver, it did not mean the Pettys were better than anyone else. What they did was a job, like a farmer or a police officer or a construction worker—no better, no worse. If his parents ever caught Kyle bragging, he would be punished severely.

Kyle took these lessons very seriously. In fact, when the Pettys were summoned to the White House in 1971 and Kyle met President Richard M. Nixon, he did not tell anyone. When the local newspaper ran a story and a picture a few days later, his teacher and classmates were shocked that he had not said anything.

The relationship between Kyle and Richard was a tricky one. Richard was very proud of Kyle but rarely praised him or told him how much he loved him. Everyone else in the racing business knew how Richard felt about his son, but the King had a lot of trouble expressing himself. The Petty family was not a kissing and hugging family.

Richard looks in on Kyle, who beams with excitement after his first run on a superspeedway.

The Petty clan gathers on the victory stand to celebrate Kyle's stunning win at the 1979 ARCA 200.

Lee may never have told Richard and Maurice how proud he was of them, but over time they came to understand that he was. Richard was the same way with Kyle. But like Richard's mom, Kyle's mom gave him plenty of loving and always told him how his father felt.

"I'm not an emotional person," Richard admits. "That's a real big fault of mine. When Kyle wins a race, I just beam. But I don't tell him. His mother, though, she pats him all the time."

The beaming began with Kyle's first race on a closed course, at the 1979 ARCA 200 in Daytona. In one of the lower-tier races held during the week leading to the Daytona 500, Kyle took a boxy, year-old Dodge Magnum off the family scrap heap and amazed the racing world with a gritty victory. In 1980, Kyle started 14 Winston Cup races for Petty Enterprises and became a regular for the team in 1981.

Though humble and respectful of the older drivers, Kyle understood the importance of creating an image for the fans and looked more to the future than to the past. "Growing up, I didn't really pay attention to the history stuff," he admits.

Over the next decade, Kyle and Richard raced with and against each other 20 to 30 times a year. Richard won three events in 1983 and two more in 1984 to reach 200 career victories. Although he continued driving right through the 1992 season, he did not win another Winston Cup race. The 1987 season marked the last time Richard

LUCKY SEVEN

In 1981, Richard won his seventh and final Daytona 500 to establish a record that is unlikely to be broken. It was a masterful race, as Richard gained a 10-second lead over Bobby Allison with a lightning-quick pit stop and then held on to edge his old rival by just four seconds. Dale Inman had calculated to the drop how much gas Richard needed. He ran out just as he crossed the finish line!

Just as Richard had quickly distinguished himself from Lee, Kyle drew clear lines between himself and Richard. He was one of NASCAR's new breed of drivers. Stock-car racing was entering a new era, and it paid to get noticed. Kyle was a very stylish dresser, and his trademark ponytail made him instantly recognizable. Where Richard was quiet and reserved, Kyle was quick with a joke or hilarious story. He even recorded a country music album.

Richard hoists up his grandson, Adam, so he can catch all the action. Adam would grow up to become the family's fourth-generation race-winner.

Kyle gets a kiss from his wife, Patti, after his first Winston Cup victory.

finished in the Top 10 of the Winston Cup standings.

In the mid-1980s, with retirement on the horizon, Richard began to get more serious about running a racing team. For two years, he left Petty Enterprises, then returned in 1986 with cousin Dale Inman to rebuild the family business. Petty Enterprises actually shut down for several months in 1985, after Maurice retired. By this time, Kyle was driving for the Wood brothers, a team that had put racing legends such as David Pearson, Cale Yarborough, and Neil Bonnett behind the wheel of their cars.

Driving for the Wood brothers in 1986, Kyle won his first Winston Cup event at Richmond, Virginia. It marked the first time in history that three generations of drivers had won elite-level events. Unfortunately, it was not the glorious breakthrough victory he had hoped for. Kyle was running fifth with three laps to go when the two leaders, Dale Earnhardt and Darrell Waltrip, got tangled up and started a chain reaction of accidents. As Kyle picked his way through the smoking wrecks, he realized that the third- and fourth-place cars had plowed into the debris and were out of the race, too. He floored it and cruised home to an easy victory.

After the race, Kyle was asked to analyze his improbable win. "I put on new underwear this morning," he joked. Kyle knew the underwear had nothing to do with his first-place finish. But just in case, he wore the same pair for the rest of the season! Kyle won the Coca-Cola 600 in 1987 for his second career vic-

In the 1993 book *Kyle at 200 M.P.H.,* Kyle gave fans an inside look at the Petty family.

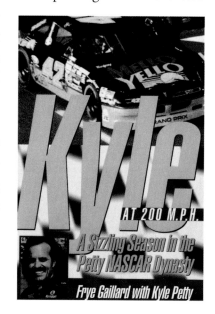

tory. That win gave him enough points to finish ahead of Richard, who ended the season ranked eighth. It was the one and only time father and son finished in the Top 10.

The most memorable moment for the Pettys during the 1980s was also the scariest. Over the course of his career, Richard had broken a lot of bones and suffered from stomach ulcers. But in more than 1,000 starts, he had somehow managed to avoid that one horrifying wreck that sooner or later seems to catch up with every driver. During the 1988 Daytona 500, Richard's luck ran out.

Coming out of turn four on the race's 106th lap, Richard was bumped from behind by Phil Barkdoll, causing him to collide with A. J. Foyt. In full view of the main grandstand, car number 43 suddenly went airborne, floating and turning for a sickening second before slamming into the track at 180 mph.

From there, it got worse. Richard grabbed the steering wheel and held on tight as his Pontiac Grand Prix did several pirouettes on its front grill, then rolled six times. The force

Richard's car begins to disintegrate after tumbling several times and hitting the wall at the 1988 Daytona 500. Crew chief Dale Inman thought the King was dead after this crash.

Richard takes the checkered flag at the 1984 Firecracker 400. It was the 200th and final victory of his career.

sheared off bits of rubber and metal, which sprayed in all directions. Luckily, a reinforced mesh screen had just been installed for the race, so no spectators were injured. Richard lay motionless as his car finally came to a halt. Everyone strained to see if he was still in one piece when Brett Bodine, hoping to slither through the debris from the accident, cut a tire and slammed into Richard at full speed. Fans screamed in terror as the shattered hulk of Richard's car was spun violently into the concrete wall.

Dale Inman, Richard's crew chief, pressed the talk button on his radio, knowing it was unlikely Richard would be conscious, or even alive. "You all right?" he asked. Incredibly, Inman got a response. "I'll talk to you when I get my breath."

A short time later, Richard walked into the local hospital. A few hours later he walked out. He had survived one of the most terrible crashes in history with a sprained ankle. "If there had been a long enough caution," he jokes, "we could have gotten back and finished the race!"

KYLE

BY THE NUMBERS
THROUGH 2000

STARTS	585
WINS	8
TOP 10S	167
CHAMPIONSHIPS	0
CAREER EARNINGS	$12,262,053

MOVING OVER, STEPPING UP

chapter 7

"I'm stepping down, boy,
so now it's your turn
to go do it."

Richard Petty

The final decade of the 20th century was a special one for the Pettys and their fans. During the 1990s, three generations climbed behind the wheels of stock cars and put the pedal to the metal. Richard's final three years as a driver, 1990–92, were solid but unspectacular. Still, he started 29 races each season and finished each year ranked among the Top 30.

Richard called his final season a "Fan Appreciation Tour," but it was the fans who came out by the millions to get a final glimpse of the King. It was not an easy time for Richard. When you have spent so much time in the

> ### DID YOU KNOW?
>
> Though he soon got used to being a team owner, Richard found that it was a waste of time trying to coach other drivers. "Most things a racer learns," he says, "he learns on his own. It's called 'seat time.'"

Richard embraces his wife, Lynda, prior to his final race, the 1,184th of his career.

Richard was unable to finish his last race, the 1992 Hooters 500.

driver's seat, giving it up can feel like dying. His final race was in Atlanta on November 14. Prior to the race, 75,000 people came to a special concert in the Georgia Dome to watch the group Alabama give Richard a memorable musical goodbye.

The 1990s were very good to Kyle. In 1992, he became the first member of his family to earn $1 million in prize money during a single season. He formed a very successful relationship with team owner Felix Sabates and won six races. For a time, Sabates was like a second father to Kyle. After the 1996 season, Kyle and Sabates parted. Kyle became a partner with Richard and engine builder Dick Evans in the "new" Petty Enterprises racing team, called PE2.

The team put two drivers on the track—Kyle and someone else. The problem was, whoever that "someone else" was, they tended to disappear in Richard's long shadow. Bobby Hamilton, who drove for the team over three seasons, was a good example. When he won at Rockingham in 1997, the headlines read "King Returns to Victory Lane." Hamilton quit and was replaced by Michael Andretti, the nephew of Mario Andretti, one of history's most successful drivers. Yet even the Andretti name could not keep him from being obscured by the Petty mystique.

The answer to this problem turned out to be right under the Pettys' noses. Who better to drive for Petty Enterprises than another Petty? Kyle's oldest son, Adam, was

DID YOU KNOW?

When Adam Petty started racing on the ASA circuit in 1997, he became the country's first fourth-generation professional athlete. He appeared on a special commemorative phone card with his father and grandfather, issued by Sprint.

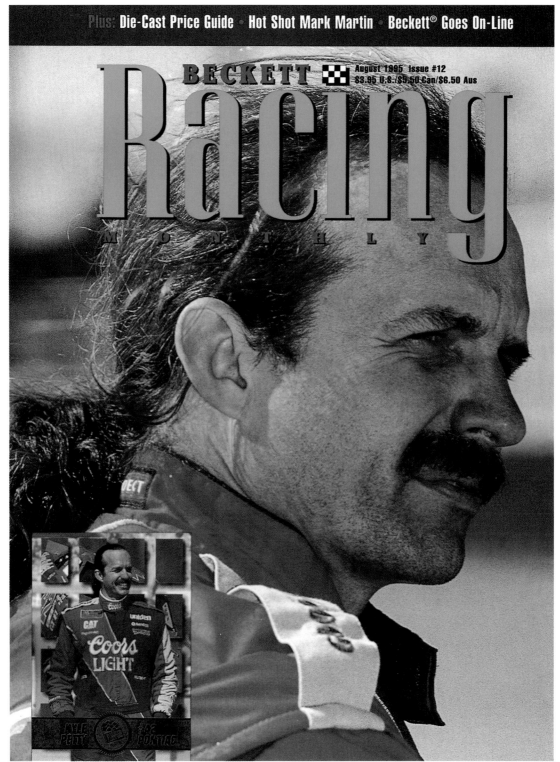

Plus: **Die-Cast Price Guide** • **Hot Shot Mark Martin** • **Beckett® Goes On-Line**

BECKETT 🏁 August 1995 Issue #12
$3.95 U.S./$5.50 Can/$6.50 Aus

Racing
MONTHLY

KYLE PETTY #42 PONTIAC

By the time Kyle appeared on this 1995 magazine cover,
he was a stock-car legend in his own right.

Richard and Kyle celebrate with Adam after his first win on a superspeedway, in 1998. The future looked bright for the Petty clan.

having good success racing old stock cars on the American Speed Association (ASA) circuit. Just 17, he seemed to have the family gift for running aggressive, intelligent races. Richard vowed not to rush him to Winston Cup, however. Looking back, he feels that he pushed his own son into the top level of racing way too soon. Looking back himself, Kyle now agrees. "That was a failed experiment from the beginning," he says.

Adam, it was decided, would serve his apprenticeship in the Busch series, a tier below Winston Cup competition. If and when he proved himself ready to handle racing's top level, then he would take his place in the family business. On September 30, 1998, Adam took a major step toward joining the Petty team when he won the 100-mile ARCA event at the Charlotte Motor Speedway. Winning a race on one of the superspeedways is a must before moving up to face the top competition, and at 18, Adam had that crucial win under his belt.

After the race, Kyle said that of all the wins the Petty clan had registered over the

> **DID YOU KNOW?**
>
> Adam's victory in his first ARCA start reminded everyone of Kyle's brilliant debut at the same age, back in 1979. When they checked the record books, they found that Adam was now the youngest ARCA winner—beating Kyle's record by five months.

years, this one made him the proudest. Adam was asked how he felt when he heard these words. "It makes me want to cry," he replied.

Adam watches as Richard and Kyle inspect his car prior to a
practice run in Concord, North Carolina.

SO GOOD, SO FAST, SO YOUNG

chapter **8**

> **"Losing family members is
> a part of life, but it doesn't
> make it any easier."**
>
> *Richard Petty*

n Adam, Kyle saw a lot of what his father was, and what he was *not*. The kid had that special something that great race drivers have: focus and desire. Richard agreed. "When Kyle came along," he remembers, "he wanted to drive a race car, but he also wanted to ride his motorcycles, play his guitars, get married the first thing—all sorts of stuff."

Like Kyle, Adam had developed an interest in racing early. He was three when Kyle bought him a three-wheel ATV, and

> **"Racing in my family is probably like how other families teach their kids to swim— throw them in the water and let them do it. I remember when my dad set me on that three-wheeler for the first time. Before long I was doing donuts and popping wheelies!"**
>
> ADAM PETTY

The relationship between Adam and his grandfather was a special one. They shared
an intense passion for racing that Kyle never really felt.

within a year he had broken his collarbone. By the age of six, Adam was driving go-
karts in local competitions. At 12, he was racing mini sprint cars and entered the
Legends Car Competition at 15, lying about his age (and driver's license!) to qualify.
With the help of a tutor he roared through high school in three years so he could start
full-time racing sooner and spent his nights working on engines as far back as he
could remember.

Adam had a special relationship with his grandfather. Although born more than 40
years apart, they seemed to speak the same language and share the same thoughts.
Often, they would go for long walks on the family compound. With happiness and a
little jealousy, Kyle (whose relationship with his son was always more like two buddies
than a parent and child) often observed that Adam was the "son" his own father never
really had.

Adam had something else in common with his famous grandfather. A few weeks before Adam's win at Charlotte, he was competing in an ASA race near St. Paul, Minnesota. During a pit stop his crew chief, Chris Bradley, decided to make a quick adjustment to the sway bar while the car was on jacks for a tire change. Bradley did not tell anyone what he was doing, figuring that he would get in and out in a couple of seconds.

The adjustment took longer than he expected, however, and the jackman let the car down, not realizing Bradley was underneath. Adam, who had been trained to hit the accelerator the instant the tires hit the ground, took off and crushed his crew chief, killing him. Adam was not sure what he had run over and did not know anything was wrong until the race was stopped.

Adam was devastated. Kyle did not know what to say. "His moods changed from day to day, almost hour to hour," his father says. "There wasn't a lot I could say because I'd never been through anything like that."

Richard had. When Adam returned home, his grandfather sat him down, told him about the boy who had died at the drag strip in Georgia, and explained that there was nothing he could have done differently. Also, Richard's brother-in-law had been killed a generation earlier in a pit-stop mishap. It was just bad luck. These things were part of racing—either the guilt and sorrow will destroy you, or you will overcome it and be stronger, Richard said. The talk did wonders for Adam. Later, he would say that he had gone to Minnesota a boy but had come back a man.

Adam got his first ride in a Busch series event that October and did well. During the 1999 season, he raced full-time and made 42 starts, with four Top 10 finishes. After the 1999 season, the Pettys put their heads together and decided that Adam needed another year on the Busch circuit. During the 2000 season, Richard and

> ## DID YOU KNOW?
>
> Adam's first career victory came on June 27, 1998, on a short track near Kansas City, Missouri. At 18, he became the youngest ASA winner, breaking a record set by Mark Martin. Though Adam drove well that day, it was a series of brilliant pit calls by crew chief Chris Bradley that enabled him to make up a two-lap deficit.

Kyle promised, they would work him into a couple of Winston Cup events. They explained to him that Petty Enterprises would one day be his to run and that he had to learn to take things one step at a time.

True to their word, Adam found himself behind the wheel of a Petty Enterprises car for his Winston Cup debut in April of 2000 at the Texas Motor Speedway. Sadly, Richard could not be there to witness the historic moment; Lee Petty, old and frail, was losing his fight with a severe stomach disorder and needed his son by his side. Kyle was in Texas, though. In fact, he agreed to enter the race as a substitute driver for the Wood brothers. When the race ended, he finished one spot ahead of his son, in 39th place. The thrill of Adam's first Winston Cup race was dampened by the sad news that came a few days later. Adam's great-grandfather, Lee, had passed away.

Although Adam had finished far off the pace in Texas, he had driven well enough to earn another Winston Cup start. He was to enter the prestigious Coca-Cola 600 in Charlotte over Memorial Day weekend, but first there was a Busch race in Loudon, New Hampshire, to attend to. The Friday before the race, Adam climbed into his car for a practice run. Drivers do this to get the feel of the course and the feel of the car so they can make final adjustments.

As Adam built up speed, everything seemed to be working fine. Alone on the track, he began to push his car hard. Streaking into a turn at 150 mph, something went terribly wrong. The accelerator got stuck, and in the second separating him from disaster he was unable to kill the engine and steer out of danger. A 3,400-pound car smashing into a concrete wall at that speed creates a force on the human body 50 to 75 times the force of gravity. There is no way in the world that a driver can survive a crash like this.

Adam Petty was gone.

"I've always sort of believed that whatever happens was meant to happen, and that such things are part of life," says Richard. "It was Adam's time and he's not here anymore."

DID YOU KNOW?

An eerily similar crash on the very same track where Adam was killed also took the life of Kenny Irwin (right). The deaths of these young drivers led immediately to new rules on engine cut-off switches and convinced NASCAR to investigate replacing its concrete walls with safer materials.

The racing world came together on May 15, 2000, to mourn the death of racing's most promising young star.

In their grief, Kyle and Richard turned to what they knew best: their work and their family. The Petty clan pulled together and tried to sort out the tragedy, then got back to the business of racing. Adam's father drove in his place and finished the season for Petty Enterprises, while Richard set about the task of reformulating plans for the family business.

"We had to reevaluate things because as everybody knows, we were putting a lot of future and a lot of things in the basket with Adam to sort of carry the torch for us," says Richard. "It may take us a little bit of time before we get everything figured out."

After Adam's death, Kyle announced that he would finish the season in his son's place.

Some within the racing world believe that, without the family's patriarch (Lee) and its future (Adam), Richard and Kyle will drift away from the sport and close down Petty Enterprises. Richard insists they will not. "Petty Enterprises will continue as it always has," he says. "Racing went on before the Pettys, and it will go on after the Pettys. But the Pettys have to make a living somewhere, and racing is what they know best. And that's what they're going to be doing."

Whatever father and son decide to do, and wherever life takes them, they will never lose sight of what is important. Once so different, Richard and Kyle have become more and more alike with each passing year. It has even become a family joke. That's good, because in the end, they are family. They are Pettys.

And if racing is truly in their blood, then so be it. Race they will. If not, that's okay, too. Deep down, they have all they ever expected or hoped for.

They have each other.

How much longer will Kyle continue to race? No one is sure.
But one way or another, he says, Petty Enterprises will go on.

Adam and Lee may be gone, but fans will never forget them.

INDEX